r

ANATOMY LESSON

MATT SPADAFORA

ANATOMY LESSON

Stories

Life Rattle Press, Toronto, Canada

Published in Canada by Life Rattle Press
Toronto, ON
www.liferattle.ca

Spadafora, Matt
Anatomy Lesson
ISBN: 978-1-927023-69-3
Life Rattle Press New Publishers Series

Printed and bound in the United States

TABLE OF CONTENTS

For Mom & Dad.

INTRODUCTION

When I tell people the concept of my book is a series of short stories centered around different parts of my body, I always hastily add, "but it isn't as dirty as you are probably thinking it will be." Allow me to say right now: there is no story in this book entitled "Penis." So don't worry, Mom.

I am very privileged to have taken the Making a Book course that allowed me to create this project. I sometimes doubt my choice in university, but then I remember that I am incredibly thankful to have happened upon the Professional Writing & Communication program, to have taken this course with this amazing opportunity, and to have been taught by Guy Allen. I never thought I'd get to a point as a writer where I was able to create something from scratch and to then hold it in my hands as a real piece of work, and I am incredibly humbled by it. And to Guy Allen: you have taught me so much about writing. I could not say thank you enough.

You may think to yourself, "writing a book seems like a huge undertaking," and by God, you'd be right. And yet, because I am a master in procrastination, I did not start work on this book until January of 2014, even though I was enrolled in the class for close to a year before the start of the semester. I am proud of the work I have done in this book, but I can't help but think what it might have looked like if I devoted more time to it. But hey, I'm damn proud.

The idea struck me amidst my sleeplessness. The original concept for this book was to be an autobiography written in the style of Tina Fey's *Bossypants*. For some reason, it never clicked. I'd write, I'd write some more, and then I would delete what I had. Maybe it's because I'm not meant to write an autobiography. Maybe it's because, deep down, I knew that my life is just not noteworthy enough to warrant an autobiography at twenty-two years of age. It was late December, and I told myself that this book had to be a collection of short stories, but I didn't know what it would be or how I would do it. I'm most comfortable with creative non-fiction, which is the primary focus of the Professional Writing program. I thought, well, I could potentially incorporate some of the stories I've already handed in for class!

Naturally, none of these stories are from any of my classes.

It was around 4am on one of my most sleepless nights when the idea struck me: *what if I wrote stories centered around my body?*

And then everything clicked.

I knew immediately that I would write about my tattoo, about the time I broke my foot, about an abysmal Valentine's Day that I've kept close as one of my most quintessential Matt stories, and I knew that I could make these stories my entries for "Leg," for "Foot," and for "Heart," respectively. I sat upright in bed with a new note open on my iPod and listed a bunch of body parts—"Penis" never made it to the list—and started to associate potential stories to each of my parts. I think it worked well as a framing device, and what you have now in your hands is a collection of weird, weird situations that happen to directly impact any given part of my body.

You'll find, in this book, that I'm a loser. One of the most important lessons I learned when writing portfolios about myself for class is that nobody likes to read about someone whose life is perfect. Readers want the underdog; readers want to associate with someone they can root for, with someone who's endearingly pathetic, in some way. I can't say you'll want to root for me, but I like to think I'm endearingly pathetic.

And so you might find yourself in me when you read about this one time when I pissed myself in public, or when I got hammered and injured myself.

But you might also find yourself relating when I talk about my depression, or about how I've dealt with the issues of body image while growing up.

I personally thank you for supporting me and this project. I'm lucky to have found my passion in life (writing, if that wasn't clear), and I'm even luckier to have readers such as you to make what I do worth it.

Much love.

Take care.

Matt

HEAD

Get up.

I'm glued to my mattress. I lay atop my comforter in nothing but a pair of boxers and a navy University of Toronto t-shirt with a hole in its side. My head pounds. My stomach growls. I have no appetite. *It'd be a good idea, going to the cafeteria*, I tell myself. *Get yourself up. See some people.*

Find a reason to smile.

I swing my legs to the side. My feet meet the pile of clothes on the floor between my bed and my desk. I dig through the pile and find my favourite pair of sweatpants, a navy UofT pair, with two growing holes on the right knee.

I step into the sweatpants and pull my arms through the holes of my red Residence Life Staff hoodie.

I catch my reflection in the full-length mirror on my closet door.

The person I see looking back doesn't look at all like someone I'd want to be friends with. His curly hair sticks out in every direction, heavy, weighted down by leftover hair gel from the day before that he probably didn't bother to wash out in the shower this morning. The dark circles under his eyes stand out like they were slapped on with black face paint. Two-day-old stubble stretched across his jaw, and he itches his chin at the same time as I do. With a drawn out sigh, I leave my friend in the mirror.

My Blackberry vibrates and the light flashes purple. Purple is the colour I've assigned to Kristen. I can't even remember what we've been talking about today. I smile at the purple light. It makes me feel comfortable. I decide to check the message later.

I grab my brown leather jacket from the back of a chair in my living room and slip my feet into an old pair of Under Armour flip-flops. I wiggle my toes against the tight strap over the bridge of my foot.

The brisk outdoor air helps my headache. I walk from my building to Oscar Peterson Hall, the first-year residence apartment with the main cafeteria and the Student Housing & Residence Life office. My flip-flops chomp the gravel path. I pass a first-year student on the bridge. The wood beneath my feet sags with dampness left over from the downpour the night before.

I pull the heavy door and a blast of warm air hits blows against my face. I force my keycard into the slot in the door to the Student Housing office and push down on the handle when the light flashes green. On the other side of the door I hear boisterous laughter and too many conversations happening at once.

Go in there, says one voice in my mind.

There are a few people you'd like to avoid right now, says another.

I shut the door. I stuff my key into my jacket pocket and turn toward the cafeteria.

"Hey!" says my friend Chris from across the OPH lobby. *Look happy.* I try to force a smile. It's around noon, meaning that other Dons and delegates from Residence Council are tabling for various events. I raise my right hand and wave at Chris and our friend Riley, who sits behind one of the tables. The large banner on the windows behind him reads "Movember" and is decorated with a large painted mustache. Paper mustaches on Popsicle sticks, "I Heart Mo" stickers, and a donation box cover the table in front of him.

Chris opens his arms up for a hug. At nearly a foot taller than him I feel like I'm smothering him when I hug him back. "How you doing, big guy?"

"You look tired," Riley says. The red mustache growing above his upper lip looks out of place. *Happy Movember.*

"I'm not tired."

"Then you look sad."

"I'm not sad either," I lie.

Chris looks up at me. "You sure you're okay?"

"Yup. I'm fine. I'm just grabbing something to eat. Really hungry. I'll see you on my way out."

I walk into the cafeteria. I keep my head down. I don't want to see anyone else I know. I don't want to have to pretend to be in a good mood to make sure I'm not concerning them.

Nothing for lunch interests me. My stomach growls again. I haven't eaten since last night. The synthetic smells in the air of cafeteria sauces and meats make me nauseous. My headache worsens. I leave empty handed. *Eat later. You've gotta eat.*

Chris and Riley both smile at me when I emerge from the cafeteria. *They know you're not happy. Convince them.*

"Garbage," I say, pointing over my shoulder. "As usual, am I right?" I laugh.

Chris stands up and grabs me into another hug. "Let's hang out later, big guy," he says. "We'll hang out and talk about stuff. I'll text you later. Don't forget on me."

"Alright. Okay."

"Hey Matt," Riley says, "wanna know something funny?"

"Eh," I say. I don't feel like laughing at his ridiculous humour today. "Maybe not." I walk away.

"It's funny, I swear!"

"I believe you," I call back.

The wind picks up. I hug my chest. I swipe my card at the back door of Erindale Hall, climb a flight of stairs, walk down the hall, and enter my unit. I unzip my sweater and kick my sweatpants off before I make it into my bedroom. The mattress sags when I sit on it.

I browse Facebook and text Kristen a bunch of times about nothing. She makes me laugh a few times before I realize that all I really want to do is sleep. I have class in three hours but I have no desire to go. I toss my MacBook onto the floor. It lands with a soft *thud* on the heap of graphic t-shirts.

I lay back down on top of my comforter. The fan starts again and the heat returns.

I turn on my side and curl my legs up. I grab my teddy bear, a ratty stuffed bear named Teddy as old as I am and as weathered as I feel, and hug him against my body.

My mind doesn't stop when I shut my eyes. I rifle through regrets, through disappointments and failed expectations and opportunities I left idle, reliving uncomfortable conversations with others, picturing faces and tears.

ANATOMY LESSON

The fan switches to heat.
After a while, I find sleep.

EARS

A breeze blows between the line of portables. Sharp November air cuts through the scratchy green wool of the Notre Dame uniform sweater stretched across my torso and pricks the back of my neck. I turn my back to the wind, hunch my shoulders, and hug my American History textbook close to my chest.

The wind picks up again. It catches Devan's green tartan kilt. She presses her kilt down and pulls her green socks over her bare knees. "Mrs. Obrovac is always late," she huffs, glaring at the closed door of Portable 16.

My empty stomach growls. *Only one more class until lunch...*

"How're you doing on the essay?" I ask Devan.

"Ugh!" she says. "I have no idea where to start. There's too much to talk about. The Kennedys were so messed up, you know? I don't know what to argue about them. How's yours going?"

I hear snickering behind me.

"Huh?"

"Your essay," Devan says. "How's it going?"

I look over my shoulder and see a group of guys standing a few feet away from Devan and I. Billy and Alex look straight at me, their mouths stretched into smirks. Other guys in our grade stand in a huddle behind them. Billy turns to Alex and laughs. I went to elementary school with both of them. I used to be friends with Alex. By the time we got to high school we stopped talking. Billy and Alex play football. I'm in the school musical.

"Matt?"

I turn back to Devan. "Oh, right, it's fine. Hey, I forgot to tell you, my mom has a book about the Kennedy scandals. If I find it I could lend it to you."

"That'd be lovely, friend!"

"Hey Matt," Billy whispers. "*Psst.*"

More snickering.

"Would you want to go to Central Library this week-end?" Devan asks. "We could get all the books we need, get started on our theses…"

"*Psst.*"

Snickers.

"I could use that," I tell Devan.

"*Psst.*"

"Hey Matt, is it true?" Billy says.

The wind blows against my neck.

I close my eyes and exhale. "Is *what* true?" I say, turning to Billy and Alex.

Billy laughs. His boisterous laughter, the same laughter that has annoyed me since we were in elementary school, echoes against the steel siding of the portables around us. The acne across Billy's cheeks contracts when he laughs.

"You know," says Alex. "So is it true?" A smile spreads across his fat face. He crosses his arms across his chest. The thick muscles in his arms bulge. Steroids. *Probably.* The guys on the football team all use them.

I remember when we used to hang out at Alex's house or at the park. I remember how much of a big deal his birthday parties were, because only the most elite people in our grade would be invited. I was never on the first tier of invited. *You're only invited if someone else couldn't make it*, he'd say. Besides that, besides everyone else in our grade caring, we were friends.

"No, Alex, I don't know what you're talking about."

"We think you do," Billy says. The group of boys laughs again.

Mrs. Obrovac rushes toward the portable. "Sorry, I'm sorry," she says. She adjusts her red glasses and brushes the cheaply dyed blonde hair out of her face blown out of place by the wind. She clutches a file bursting with loose pages against her chest with her left hand. Her boots click against the sagging wooden stairs leading up to the portable door. Everyone in my class takes a step forward toward the door. Devan's shoulder pushes into the middle of my arm.

Mrs. Obrovac fumbles through the pockets of her puffy winter jacket with her free hand. She retrieves her keys and stabs at the lock on the door. She turns against a gust of wind. "Everyone inside," she says.

I follow Devan up the three stairs. The toe of my black sneaker catches against the metal bar bridging the sagging wood and linoleum floor of the classroom. I stumble forward into the heat of the room. From outside, Alex and Billy laugh.

I take my seat in the desk behind Devan. I slam my American History textbook down onto my desk. Our friend Danielle sits at the desk across the aisle to my left. I make a silly face at her. "How're you doing?" I ask her.

"Good. Stressed." Her long straight crimson hair falls over her shoulders.

Devan turns around in her seat. "We're thinking of going to Central this weekend to work on our essays. Wanna come?"

"Sure! We need to get started on our English seminar, too," Danielle says. "Shit."

Alex sits at the desk to my left. Billy sits behind me. "*Psst*," they say in unison. The rest of the boys in their group from outside take seats across the classroom. They look between one another, smirking.

"Is it true?" Alex repeats.

My heart pounds. I ignore them. I unzip my tattered red backpack and dig out my Five Star notebook and black ballpoint pen. I flip open to a blank page, pull my red pen out of the pocket of my grey uniform dress pants, and write the date across the top of the page.

Mrs. Obrovac spreads her papers across her desk and runs her hands against her white blouse and black skirt. "Alright," she sighs. "Let's get started." She picks up a piece of chalk and drags it across the chalkboard.

I try my best to pay attention as Mrs. Obrovac begins her lesson. She talks about our essays. She talks about something that has to do with colonialism, or something. I keep my head down and my eyes fixed on the lined paper on my desk. I scratch black letters into the white page. I look up to the board and copy my teacher's words without thinking. Every few minutes I hear another "*psst*" from behind me. I dig the tip of my ballpoint pen deeper into the page as I write. The black ink bleeds through to the page beneath.

The minute hand on the clock drags itself slowly around in a circle.

"That's it for today," Mrs. Obrovac says finally. "You can take the rest of the period to work on whatever you have to do for me this week."

Devan drags her chair around and unloads her notebook, textbook, and loose papers onto the little free space I have on my desk. "Do you mind?" I say to her, laughing.

"You're not *actually* going to work on anything, are you?" Devan says. "We just need to make it look like we're working."

The class breaks into chatter. I drop my pen.

"Hey, Matt," Billy says.

"*What?*" I snap. I turn in my seat.

"So is it true?"

"Is *what* true?"

"*You* know."

Don't get mad. That's what they want.

"I don't know anything."

"Don't listen to them," Devan whispers to me.

Billy looks at Alex and nods. "Is it turn you're a faggot?" Alex says. They burst into laughter.

"I'm not." My voice trails.

"Yes, you are," Billy says.

"You're a faggot, right?" Alex says.

I try to say "I'm not" once more but the words get caught in my throat. I've been used to this sort of bullying for a while now. I've told myself that it doesn't matter what they think about me, that it doesn't matter that they're wrong, and that in a few years I'll forget all about bullies like these and their pathetic lives. The last time I defended myself against someone who called me a faggot, they told me I wouldn't be getting so defensive if I actually wasn't gay. I've learned to take it. I've learned to take it, but I haven't learned how to not let it affect me.

I turn away from Billy. I feel him looking at the back of my head. Alex laughs beside me.

Devan asks me what's wrong, but I don't say anything.

The bell rings. "See you all tomorrow," Mrs. Obrovac says.

I stand from my seat and throw my belongings into my bag. My hands shake. I'm three inches taller than Billy, a half a foot taller than Alex, but when they stand up to leave, they make me feel so small.

I step around Billy's desk. I fix my eyes on the linoleum floor.

"Wait for me!" Devan whines. I continue toward the back of the portable.

I open the door, step out into the cold, and drag myself down the steps from the door to the gravel ground. I stand beside the wall of the portable. The rest of my class files out of the portable and pass me. I cross my arms. I try not to cry. I look down at my feet.

NOSE

I duck my head through the pouring rain. Water drips from the ends of my hair and wets the collar of my red Residence Life Staff t-shirt. Raindrops patter against the shoulders of my brown leather coat. I drag my running shoes through the puddles on the pavement of Leacock Lane. At the end of the row of townhouses on my left, thumping music echoes through the night.

Sarah approaches me. The hood of her raincoat is pulled up over her red hair and the glasses on her face are blurry with raindrops. "Thanks for getting here so quickly," I tell her. Sarah is my duty partner tonight.

"What unit is it?" she asks me.

"130. End of that line of houses" —I point ahead of me in the direction of the music—"where that music is coming from."

"I thought so. I could hear it on my way here."

I sigh. "Let's go."

I adjust the duty bag slung over my shoulder. As a Residence Don, I have to take Don-On-Duty shifts throughout the month. On duty, you cannot leave residence. You keep the duty phone with you at all times, and whenever it rings for any emergencies, you pick it up. I got a call a few minutes ago about a party happening in Leacock Lane, the residence complex I'm a Don in. I was about to go to bed.

A small group of people stands in front of Leacock Lane 130. A guy tilts his head back and blows a cloud of thick smoke into the rain. One of his friends nudges him in the side and nods toward Sarah and I. "Good evening," I say to them as we pass. The smell of marijuana cuts through the air and stings my nostrils. I raise my eyebrow. "Hopefully you're staying out of trouble."

The student mumbles something, smiles nervously, and shuffles away.

The red front door hangs open. The bass of the music shakes my chest. Through the open door, I see a packed crowd of people in the living room. I breathe in and out slowly. *This is going to be a long night.*

I ball my fist and slam it against the door. *Knock, knock,*

knock! "Don-On-Duty!" I shout into the house. A few people close to the door look up at me, but turn away.

I sigh at Sarah. She knocks on the door. *Knock, knock, knock!* "DON-ON-DUTY!" we shout in unison. Heads snap up and eyes widen. People push into each other toward and start to rush out of the door at the back of the living room.

A girl rounds the corner and appears in front of Sarah and I. "Hi," she says. Her eyes are red and her cheeks are wet with tears. "I'm the one who called."

"Can we come in?" I ask. We aren't allowed into student units without their permission.

"Of course," she says.

Someone shouts, "shit, the Dons are here!" The music screeches to a halt and the room continues to empty. Students I recognize as first years push past Sarah and I and pour out into the pouring rain. We are never, under any circumstance, allowed to chase after any students.

"You live here?" Sarah asks the girl.

"Uh-huh," she nods. She sniffles. Another girl with dark brown hair stands behind her with her arms crossed over her chest. "Oh, and that's my friend," the crying girl says, pointing to the brunette behind her. "She hasn't been drinking, either."

"Tell us what's happening," I say. "From the start."

"Okay. My roommate... it's her birthday, and she's

having this party. Me and my friend just got back to the house. We found a guy passed out in the middle of the room. That's when I called you."

"Let's not waste anymore time, then," I say. "Where's this guy?"

I follow the girls into the living room. The back door hangs wide open. Only a couple of people remain. A lanky guy lies face down in the middle of the floor, and a girl in pink flannel pajamas kneels beside him. Empty bottles of beer and liquor line the walls and crowd every flat surface. The air is stale. It smells like sweat and vodka.

"What happened to him?" says Sarah.

"He hasn't been drinking," the girl in the pink flannel pajamas slurs. She hiccups.

"And have you?"

"Yes." *Hiccup.* "I'm legal, though."

The guy on the floor turns his head and opens his eyes. "Hey, there," I say, leaning over him. "Are you feeling alright?"

He opens his mouth and brown vomit pours out onto the carpet. The girl in pink giggles. I gag. A sharp stench of burning and bubbling alcohol meets my nose. I press my arm against my nose and turn away. "Call Campus Police," I say to Sarah. Her face is pale. She nods at me with wide eyes, digs her phone out of the pocket of her raincoat, and disappears into the front hallway.

I kneel beside the guy on the floor. The smell of vomit churns my stomach. "Okay," I say, pinching my nose. "I'm going to put you into the recovery position, alright?"

The guy hiccups and spits out more vomit.

I blank on everything I learned in first aid. *Roll him so he's facing away from you*, I tell myself, *so that if he vomits, he's puking away from you*. I place my left hand on his shoulder and my right hand on his ribs and roll him toward me onto his side. I stretch his left arm out and lay his head against it. He coughs out more vomit. This time, the vomit is clear.

The girl in pink flannel pajamas hiccups again. She stares at me with glassy eyes. She opens her mouth to speak. Vomit cascades out of her mouth like a waterfall. The vomit stains her flannel. It pools on the carpet. The girl who called me sobs from the kitchen. "I am—not— cleaning this," she says to her friend between sobs.

Sarah returns and clasps her hands against her face. "Campus Police are coming," she says between her fingers.

"Do you live here on campus?" I ask the girl in pink.

"No."

"Do you have a way to get home?"

She pulls her phone out of the pocket on her pajama top. The top of the phone glistens with vomit. "I can call someone," she slurs. Her fingers, sticky with puke, jab at the screen.

"Does he live here?"

"I don't know him."

"He does," says the girl from the kitchen.

Another girl hops down the stairs, laughing. "How's everything down here?" she shouts. Clear alcohol spills out of the red plastic cup in her hand. A sash that reads "Happy Birthday" sits across her chest. "Oh," she says, pointing at me. "You're Matt. I'm one of Stef's students." She hiccups.

"Mhm." I try not to gag at the smell of vomit in the air.

"Is this your party?" Sarah asks her.

"Yes. I'm turning nineteen."

"She's turning eighteen," says her roommate from the kitchen.

I shut my eyes and exhale. *When are Campus Police getting here?*

"Uh, Matt," the birthday girl says. "We kinda need your help upstairs."

I shoot a worried look at Sarah. "Are you okay down here?" I ask her.

She frowns and nods quickly. "I'll be okay," she says faintly.

"Try and get as much information from the girl who called me," I say. She nods and pulls out a piece of paper from her duty bag. "Get the names of everyone, too."

I follow the birthday girl up the stairs. Her feet cross and she stumbles into the wall. I throw my hands up to catch her. "You should sit down once we're upstairs," I tell her.

I step onto the upstairs landing. Three guys stand against the wall. They try to hide their bottles of beer behind their backs. "The party is over," I say to them, pointing at the stairs. "Out."

"They're with me," the birthday girl says. "And they're with the other guy, too."

"What other guy?"

She stumbles toward one of the bedrooms and presses her hands against the door. The white door swings. "He needs your help," she tells me. My heart pounds. I step toward the open door and squint. I can't see anything in the darkness. I flick on the light.

The stench of vomit greets me. I turn away from the room and suck in clean air. I open my eyes.

A guy in black sits on the edge of the bed. He stares at the wall in front of him. His mouth hangs open. His eyes look dead. Brown vomit trickles down from his open mouth, stains the front of his black shirt, and pools in a puddle around his feet. A heavy puddle of vomit sits in the middle of the comforter on the bed. Streaks of puke smear across the light green walls beside him.

I snap my fingers toward him. "Hello," I say. He doesn't move. "Are you alright?"

"He's cool," says one of the guys on the landing. "We're

just leaving."

I hold my palm out to him. "You're not going anywhere with this guy. He's clearly not well. We're waiting until Campus Police get here."

"I'll just take him home, man," the guy says.

"Sit down."

"Matt!" Sarah calls from downstairs. "The officers are here!"

I turn to the birthday girl. "You," I say, pointing at her, "are coming downstairs with me. And you're setting that"—I point at her red plastic cup—"down."

I lead the way back down the stairs. I take a deep breath. I pinch my nose to block the smell of alcohol and vomit waiting for me at the bottom of the stairs. Two EMS in red shirts kneel beside the guy face down on the ground. A male Campus Police officer nods as Sarah speaks to him, scribbling notes onto his notepad. A female officer questions the girl who called me. I lean back against the wall. I rub my eyes.

It's going to be a long night.

HEART

I pull the door open and step into a blast of warmth from the heaters above. I brush snow off my shoulders, rub my feet across the soaked mat on the floor, and kick slush from the toes of my camel boots. My hand is tightly wrapped around a folded pink piece of paper.

I step through a second door into The Spectrum. The Spectrum, Notre Dame Catholic Secondary School's two-story atrium, is the heart of my high school. During the week, The Spec bustles with students in grey dress slacks, deep green sweaters, and white dress shirts and blouses with a green "ND" embroidered over the heart. Today, a Saturday morning, The Spec sits still. With only a week before opening night, Mr. Martino insisted our production of *Pride & Prejudice* was in such rough shape that we needed an all-day weekend rehearsal.

Today also happens to be Valentine's Day.

I run my fingers over the crease of the folded paper in my hand. The edge sharpens. The corners of the page dig into my fingertips. I press the paper between my palms, smoothing the surface. I turn it over. Black cursive writing is etched across the pink surface. It reads Her name.

I turn down a hallway lined with blue lockers. I pass a set of doors to the empty cafeteria, walk beside an empty display case in the wall, and reach my locker.

My fingers slip on the lock. The door squeals open. I toss my jacket onto the heap of crumpled papers and textbooks at the bottom of the locker. For a second, I hesitate. *Throw it into the locker and forget about it.* The paper twists in my hands.

Instead, I grab the bound *Pride & Prejudice* script from the shelf level with my face.

Feet slam on the tiles behind me. The paper is wrenched from my hands. I spin. Devan and Kim dash past me with a "hey Matt!" Devan holds the pink paper above her head in triumph. She reaches the end of the hall and takes a right into the drama hallway. I drop my script, slam my locker shut, push the lock back together, and break into a run after them.

"Give it back!" I call. My voice bounces through the empty hallways.

I turn right. Devan and Kim run past two girls kneeling over a long brown banner in the middle of the hallway with paintbrushes in their hands. They reach the end of the hall and collapse on the ground. I jog past the banner on the ground and nearly kick over a plastic cup filled with red paint.

Devan unfolds the paper and begins to read. Kim hangs over her shoulder.

"Give it back," I say again. I hold out my hand. Devan turns away.

"This is so nice," she says.

"Shut up."

Kim looks up at me and smiles. "This is adorable."

"It's not for you."

"'Your smile makes me smile,'" Devan reads out loud.

"Shut *up*."

"Are you really going to give it to her?"

"That's the *plan*." I grab at the paper. Devan blocks me again.

"She'll like it," says Kim.

"Hey guys," says a voice behind me. "What are you looking at?"

My blood runs cold. Devan and Kim freeze.

I turn slowly. "Oh, hey," I say to Her. My cheeks flush.

Her curly hair lies damp from fallen snow. The mist on her glasses slowly fades away, revealing the blue eyes behind the glass. She smiles at me.

"What's that?" she says, nodding toward the paper in Devan's hands.

"Nothing," I say quickly.

Devan and Kim stand up. Devan forces the paper into my clenched fist. "We're just… we're just leaving," she says, taking off into a jog down the hall and out of sight.

"Um… bye," Kim says, following Devan around the corner. I hear their footsteps quicken in pace down the hall.

"This is for you," I say suddenly, forcing the pink paper out toward her. The paper is crumpled in my hand. She takes it. "Uh, Happy Valentine's Day."

"Oh," she says. She unfolds the paper and reads. Her eyes dart back and forth. I shut my eyes. My cheeks burn even hotter. *Stupid. I should've left it in my locker, or at home on my desk, or maybe I should never have written it in the first place. Stupid, stupid.*

"This is nice," she says finally.

"Yeah, uh, you're cool, and stuff."

Silence hangs between us.

She opens her arms up for a hug. I approach her slowly. I wrap my arms around her body and hold her for only a second before I let go. I look down at my boots. The light brown material is stained dark by slush.

"Alright, well… I gotta go," I say.

"Me too."

"I'll see you in a few minutes, I guess. At rehearsal."

"Yeah. At rehearsal."

"I need to get my script."

"Me too."

"Happy, uh… never mind. Have a good day." I walk past her, back the way I came. I pass the girls painting on the banner paper. They don't look up. *How much did they hear?* I keep my head down as I walk. I follow the lines of grout between the tiles and turn left at the next hallway.

Devan stands by my locker. She looks up when I approach. "So?" she says. She flashes her braces at me in a smile.

I shake my head. "I need my script," I say quietly.

Devan steps aside. I reach for the lock, spin the dial, and pull. The lock doesn't budge. I try my combination again. Nothing. I pull up and down at the lock and throw it against the door. It clangs against the metal.

"That was very big of you," Devan says. "Trying that. I'm very proud of you." Her eyes water.

"I don't want to talk about it right now," I say.

"Even if it didn't go well, you tried. Did she say anything?"

"No."

"Maybe it could still turn out?"

"I don't want to talk about this. I need my script." I stare at the numbers on the lock and carefully spin the dial. I free the lock and swing the door open. I stare inside of my locker. I lean forward and press my head against the shelf level with my face. The metal edge of the shelf stings against my skin, cold. I shut my eyes and remind myself to breathe.

HANDS

I grab a handful of popcorn from the bag in my lap and shovel it into my mouth. I reach for another handful. My hand touches Katherine's. I flinch. I snap my hand away. "Sorry," she whispers over the movie.

"It's fine."

I do not like when other people eat my popcorn.

I met Katherine in passing last year. I noticed she was pretty. She lived on the same floor as some of my friends, so we talked a few times. This year, we had the same Molecular Biology class together. We talked more. I grew more attracted to her.

And then I stopped.

And when I stopped, she started.

I told myself to try, because the things about her I liked hadn't changed. I told myself I could feel the same way again.

I haven't.

She asked me to see *Harry Potter and the Deathly Hallows – Part 1* with her, even though I've already seen it once. I drove to UTM from Burlington. I picked her up in my mom's SUV. When we got to the ticket counter, I bought only one ticket.

I touch her hand again on my popcorn. I huff. She takes another handful. I fold the top of the bag, lean forward, and put the bag on the sticky theatre floor between my feet.

On the big screen, Harry follows the old woman to the attic. My heart pounds faster. Soon the old woman is going to turn into Voldemort's snake, and the music is going to scare the crap out of me like it did the first time. I grab onto the armrests and clench. I shut my eyes.

Crash! The music jolts. The snake hisses. I jump in my seat. My foot knocks the bag of popcorn over.

Katherine grabs my arm.

The snake lunges at Harry. Katherine's grip tightens on my arm. Her hands dig into my grey sweater.

Harry and Hermione escape.

Katherine's grip does not loosen.

When Harry follows the stag Patronus into the woods, Katherine's hand inches its way down my forearm. When Ron returns and he and Harry destroy Voldemort's locket with the Sword of Gryffindor, Katherine's hand slides on top of mine. When the trio visit Luna Lovegood's father and learn about the Deathly Hallows, Katherine's fingers lace through mine. When the movie reaches its climax at Malfoy Manor, the squeeze on my hand is unbearable.

The credits roll. The sconces on the walls glow. I slip my hand out of hers. I press it against my jeans, wiping away sweat.

"That was so good," Katherine says. Her blue eyes are watery. "That was sad, when Dobby died."

"Oh," I say. "Yeah. Very sad."

I stand from my seat, stretch my legs, and flex my throbbing fingers. Popcorn crunches under the soles of my Converse sneakers.

"The part with the snake was scary," she says. She stands up and pulls on her black wool jacket. She tussles her long dirty blonde hair.

"Yeah."

"I'm sorry that I grabbed onto you so hard."

"It's fine."

"I was so scared!" She laughs.

"Yup."

She follows me back to my SUV. As I drive back to UTM,

Katherine excitedly talks about the next movie. I try not to jump into the conversation even though I'm really excited about the next movie, too. *Don't seem like you're overly interested*. My hands tightly clamp the cold steering wheel.

I pull up to the front of Roy Ivor Hall. "This is you," I say.

She looks at me. I look back. We sit in silence for a minute. The engine purrs.

"That was fun," she says.

"Yes," I say. "The movie was very good."

She pauses. "I was waiting for you to ask me to see it, you know."

"Oh. Right. Sorry I didn't. Thanks for asking me, though."

The silence resumes. She leans toward me. I look at her blue eyes, at each eyelash, at the silver ring in her nose.

"I need to get back," I say. "You know. Late night. Long drive." I clench my fists on an invisible steering wheel in front of my face, make an awkward grin, and mime driving.

"Right." She unbuckles her seatbelt and throws the passenger door open. "I'll see you later, then," she says. "In a few weeks, I guess. Start of term."

"Well – I'm having my friends over to my house before school starts again. My parents are away. You should come." The words leap from my mouth. *Dammit.*

Katherine smiles. "That sounds nice!" She shuts the door behind her.

I drive home in silence.

I press my cheek against my balled fist. My head feels heavy from the beer I've drank. Devan, Kim and Danielle laugh together in the middle of my kitchen, taking pictures of one another in stupid poses with my black Nikon digital camera. Amy sits across from me at the kitchen island. Katherine sits on the stool beside me, quiet.

I had forgot I invited her to my house in Burlington when we saw the movie, so when she texted me earlier saying she was on the GO Train, I panicked. I picked her up. We shared a pizza. I counted down to the minute my friends arrived.

Kanye West's "Monster" draws to a close. "My pick," I say. I reach for my MacBook Pro and drag it across the granite countertop through the mess of empty beer bottles, empty wine bottles, empty shot glasses, and empty red plastic cups. The edge of the computer knocks a sticky ping-pong ball onto the floor. I slam my fingers onto the keys. I type "Lady Gaga" into Youtube's search bar with little precision and click the words "Lady Gaga – Paparazzi." I set the video to HD. I click full screen. I skip through the three minute introduction. The song begins.

"Yeah!" Danielle shouts. She bops her head to the music. Her dreadlocks bounce.

"No more Lady Gaga," Devan slurs.

"It's my house, and it's my pick," I say.

Katherine inches her stool closer to mine. Our legs touch. She rests her hand on the top of my thigh. Her hand is warm. My heart starts pounding. I lock eyes with Amy. Amy presses a fist against her growing smile.

Katherine and I have carried on with our weird relationship for the past few weeks. I still feel nothing. I tell myself to talk to her, to tell her that I don't feel the same way about her that she does about me. I work myself up to say it. I go out and get drunk with my friends. I text her flirty things. I wake up in the morning, mad at myself. The cycle repeats.

"She's so into you," Amy told me earlier. "It's crazy. She's cool, though."

I nodded and chugged another beer.

"I like this song," Katherine says.

No you don't. You don't like Lady Gaga.

She shifts her hand on my leg and presses harder. I ignore it.

"It's my favourite!" I shout to nobody in particular. "This is my favourite video of hers, too." I lean forward in my seat toward the screen and watch with exaggerated interest. Katherine's hand does not move. Amy continues to smirk.

I finish my warm beer. "I need another one." The empty bottle joins the collection of other empty cans of Old Milwaukee in front of me. I hop off of my stool. Katherine's hand drops. I skirt behind Kim, pull open the fridge doors, grab a cold can from the top shelf, and pop the can open with my fingers. Katherine stares at me. I look away, throw my head back, and finish half of the tall can in one gulp.

When I return to my seat, her hand finds my leg again. It stays there for the rest of the night.

Amy leaves a little bit after one in the morning. I yawn against the back of my hand. "I elect we go to bed," I say. My head is fuzzy. Devan and Kim take turns in the washroom to change into sleepwear.

Danielle curls up in the leather swivel chair beside the couch and makes a nest out of one of my comforters. "Are you going to be comfortable?" I ask her.

"Better than the floor!" she says.

"You can sleep down here," I tell Katherine. I point to the pile of pillows and blankets in a heap on the ground in front of the table. "If you want an air mattress I can get you one." I yawn again. "But we all usually find the most comfortable part of the floor and pass out."

"Dibs the couch!" Devan shouts from the washroom.

"Where are you sleeping, then?" asks Katherine.

"My bed."

"Oh." She raises her eyebrows.

She's going to follow you. Don't risk it. "Or maybe I might just… uh, stay down here."

"Can we watch a movie?"

"I'm tired."

"Let's watch a movie, Matt," Kim says from the couch.

I sigh. I kneel in front of the TV on the wall and reach down to the shelf where the DVD player sits. "We're watching *Sweeney Todd*, because it's the only DVD up here," I say.

"I love that movie," Katherine says. She grabs a blanket and two pillows and sets them down on the carpet between of the coffee table and the TV.

I flip on the TV, turn on the DVD player and press play. The movie starts. Devan flicks off the light when she returns from the washroom. I race her to the couch. The leather squeaks under me when I drop between Devan and Kim.

"Go down there," Devan hisses at me.

"No."

"There's no room for you on the couch," Kim says.

"I think Matt should come down here," Katherine says over the movie. "Beside me."

Devan stares at me. *"Go down there."*

"No."

"She wants you down there," Kim hisses.

Kim and Devan push my back. I catch myself on the edge of the table to stop from falling face first onto the floor. I turn to the two of them, my eyes wide, and I drag my finger across my throat as a threat. I shuffle around the coffee table slowly.

Katherine lies under the black and grey striped wool blanket my Nanny knit. I exhale and get down onto the floor beside her. She pats the empty pillow behind her head. I lay onto it and pull the free half of the blanket over my body.

"Well, goodnight," I whisper to her.

"You aren't going to watch the movie?"

Johnny Depp starts another song.

"I don't like this movie," I lie. "I'm not in the mood for it."

"What are you in the mood for?" She laces her fingers through mine.

"Um," I say, wrenching my hand away from hers. "Sleep. Goodnight."

I turn onto my side. My back faces her. My shoulder presses into the scratchy carpet and I sigh, thinking about my empty bed upstairs. I dig my head around in the pillow, trying to find a comfortable spot, and shut my eyes.

Katherine's arms wrap around my body from behind. She rubs her hands across my chest and stomach. I keep my eyes shut. She rubs around, inching closer to my legs. I lurch away from her. I turn onto my back, crushing her right arm under my body. I pretend to wake up from sleep. "Oh, sorry," I mumble. She retracts her arm. I pretend to fall back into sleep. She grabs onto my arm and holds my hand again.

I do not fall asleep.

My favourite song of the movie begins. *Shit, that means it's already halfway done.* Katherine has not let go of my hand. I feel her watching me. I keep my eyes glued shut.

Her hands rub across my chest and stomach again. I snort and start fake snoring. I hear her make a *tch* sound.

She grabs my wrist and raises my left arm up. She lets go of my arm. I drop it back down. She repeats the action. I start sweating. *Fuck. How would a sleeping arm react?* I concentrate on dropping my arm properly, like it would drop if I was actually unconscious. *She knows I'm awake.*

She lifts my arm and drops it again, and again. I tear my arm away from her grasp and roll over on my side once more, away from her.

She doesn't bug me again.

After an hour, I fall asleep.

STOMACH

"Everyone, go get changed. Matt, get over here."

I split from the rest of my grade seven class at the doors to the gymnasium. I shuffle toward Mr. Deluca. My feet crunch on the gravel on the schoolyard. My gym teacher glares at me. I stare at my feet.

"Can you explain yourself?" Mr. Deluca says. I look up and squint at the glare from the sun reflected on his opaque sunglasses. He folds his arms across his protruding stomach. A whistle hangs from a lanyard around his neck.

"I—I don't know what you're talking about," I say, quietly. I keep my arms pressed to my sides. My t-shirt sticks to my skin, damp with sweat.

"I watched you during the drills. You didn't do as many push-ups as everyone else. Then, you barely did as many laps as everyone when you were running. I watched. I counted."

I look back down. I want to look up at him and yell at him. I want to tell him that it isn't fair that he picks on me just because I'm not as active as the other boys in my grade. Instead I stay quiet.

"You're *lazy*," he continues. "I'm waiting for an explanation."

"The explanation is you count wrong," I say. My heart beats quickly.

"What did you say?"

"I said," my voice getting louder, "you *count wrong*. I did as much as everyone else."

"How dare you lie to me," he spits.

"I don't know what you want me to say."

His mouth hangs open. He shakes his head. "Get inside."

I jog to catch up with the class.

I push on the door to the boys' change room. I keep my head down and make a line straight for my gym bag on the bench in the corner of the room. By now, most of the other boys have changed. I sit on the bench and cross my legs. I stare down at the wood of the bench through my crossed legs, at the crude marker drawings and scratched initials. I sit silently until the rest of the boys leave, laughing with one another, not noticing me.

Then I change out of my gym clothes.

I open the door to the change room and step back into the gym. Mr. Deluca stands on the wall opposite the doors. He stares directly at me, his arms crossed. "You're going to be late for your next period," he calls. His voice echoes off of the gleaming wood floors of the basketball court and against the tall corners of the white roof. The gigantic painting of a hornet, our school's mascot, stares down at me from the wall as I pass by underneath.

"I'm coming," I shout at the front door. *Knock knock knock.* I swing the door open. Devan and Jamy smile at me.

"It's so hot," Jamy says. She steps through the door, holds her arms out, and lets out a long sigh. "The air conditioning feels so nice."

"I wouldn't know how hot it is, I've kept inside all day," I tell her.

"You have a pool," Devan says, closing the door behind her, "and you don't use it. Meanwhile people like us are melting. How is that fair?"

"That's why you're here, isn't it? Go on. Use my pool."

I follow the two girls through my foyer, down the hallway, around the island in the middle of the kitchen, and out the backdoor onto the deck my dad built when we moved here in 1995. The slowly rotting wood gently sags under my bare feet. The heat from the sun on the wood sears the bottoms of my feet. I leap across the deck onto the cooler wood under the shade cast by large umbrella drawn open above the iron patio table.

Devan and Jamy unload their bags onto chairs around the table. The patio table is tucked away in the corner of the deck and is surrounded by trellises covered in wild honeysuckle. When my dad built the deck, he put up walls of trellis to block out the view our neighbours had into our backyard for privacy. Thirteen years later, the honeysuckle he planted has choked itself in knots around the wood. Every summer, it springs back to life, only to choke itself again before the winter.

Jamy slips out of her floor length tie-dye sundress and Devan shrugs her oversized tank top over her head. "I'm wearing my gangsta bathing suit today," she says, pointing at her brown two-piece bathing suit decorated with a gold pattern she affectionately calls her "bling." Jamy reties the knot on her bathing suit at her hip.

I settle into one of the two blue Muskoka chairs I had helped put together and paint with my family when I was a kid. I push the heels of my feet into the gap between the seat and the footrest and push the footrest out with my legs. The sun slowly fries the skin on my bare legs and arms.

Devan walks up to the aboveground pool and sits on the raised ledge. My dad extended the deck when we had the pool installed so that we could walk right up to the pool. He built a couple of wooden steps leading up to the raised ledge, and connected the ladder to the steps to make it easier to get in and out.

Devan swings her legs over the ledge and into the water. "That feels so nice," she says. She pushes off into the pool and dunks her head under the water.

Jamy breaks into a run from the furthest corner of the deck. She jumps over the edge of the pool. Water splashes over the ledge and blots the light wood with dark wet spots. Water gets onto my legs. I throw my hands over my iPod and speakers sitting on the small wooden table beside my chair. "No splashing," I say. I push my iPod down onto the dock with a *click*. I press play. "Just Dance" by Lady Gaga comes on.

"Are you going to swim?" Jamy calls from the pool. She pushes her hands through her hair, slicking it back.

"Uh," I say. "No."

"You used to almost be a *lifeguard*," Devan yells. "We know you like swimming."

"Well—I—not today. I put hair gel in. I don't want to get my hair wet." I point to the curls slicked back on the top of my head.

"Come on, Matt!"

"Fine. I'll just put my legs in."

I reach into the pocket of my checkered swim shorts, grab my Ray Bans, and press them against my eyes. I hop across the deck. The wood roasting under the sun burns my feet. I sit on the ledge of the pool. I dip my feet and legs into the water. The warm water flows in a soft current around my legs. The jet under the filter always pushes the water in the pool in a clockwise current. When my sister and I found a drowned squirrel in the pool last summer, it floated clockwise in its watery grave.

Jamy, Devan and I talk for an hour. We talk about nearing the end of high school and how afraid we are for university. We talk about picking classes in a few months, and Jamy and I tell Devan that she's making the right choice with staying back at our high school for an extra semester. We tell stories to one another from last weekend when we all drank in Jamy's basement, and we laugh as we try to piece together a timeline of events with all of our fragmented points of view. We get onto the topic of talking about other people in our grade, about the people we won't miss, and about the people we will.

Jamy splashes me. The water marks my grey striped t-shirt with small, dark circles. "Aren't you hot? Jump in!" she says.

"I'm fine, I—"

Devan pushes her hands against the surface of the water and hits me with a splash. The front of my shirt sags with wetness.

I sigh and roll forward into the pool. Under the water I rustle my hands through my hair, trying to wash out as much of the hair gel as I can. I resurface and shake my wet curls out. Jamy and Devan clap. The soaked t-shirt hangs on my shoulders like a heavy curtain, but I don't take it off. "I figure I'll just keep it on since I'm already wet," I tell them. Neither of my friends question it.

I look up from my book. My mom stands in front of me. I hold my hand out in front of my face to block the sun from my eyes. "What's up?" I say.

"Aren't you going to swim?" she asks. She stands between me and the in-ground pool.

"I'm quite comfortable on this chair," I say. The coarse material digs into my lower back and into my butt. I shift my weight around. The chair digs into me whichever way I move.

My sister Alex and her friend Natalie hold underwater breathing competitions in the deep end of Natalie's pool. My dad, his friend Mike, and his friend Don—Natalie's dad—stand around the edge of the shallow end in arms reach of their beers on the cement patio around the pool. Cathy and Nancy sit on the edge of the pool near their husbands between bowls of pretzels and chips and glasses of cosmopolitans. My dad asks for another beer from the cooler. It hits the water. *Thunk*. "Nice aim," he says at someone.

"Well, why don't you take your shirt off?" my mom says. "You have a silly farmer's tan." She points at my arms. My skin is dark brown, which stands in contrast to the ghostly white of my upper arms, my shoulders, and my chest and stomach, all hidden by my black *Game of Thrones* t-shirt.

"I'm fine," I say. I look back down at my book.

"Matt," she says, her voice lowered. "It's okay if you take your shirt off. Don't worry about that here. Nobody cares about your stomach."

Natalie and Alex come up from the water, screaming and giggling and splashing each other.

"I said I'm fine."

"Don't be embarrassed, honey."

I don't answer her. My mom returns to her seat beside Nancy.

I close my book and set it down on the glass table beside me next to my warm can of Coke. I fold my arms across my stomach. *She's right. Nobody cares. Nobody cares but you. Take off your shirt and jump in the pool.*

I keep my shirt on.

72

SKIN

The sweat on my fingertips stains the top corner of the page of my book. I place the open paperback facedown on my stomach and wipe my sweaty hands against my checkered bathing suit. I trace my fingers along the crease down the center of the spine that splits the title *The Girl with the Dragon Tattoo* in two. "Come in the pool," my dad yells. I close my book and drop in into my mom's bag, reminding myself of the page I'm on. I forgot my bookmarks at home, and I refuse to fold the corner to keep my place.

I push the bridge of my aviator sunglasses against the top of my nose. I drop into the shallow end of the resort's pool. The water swallows me up over my head. I stand and shake my hair out like a dog. I drop my shoulders into the water and wade toward my dad and my sister in the center of the pool. My toes glide over light blue square tiles lining the bottom.

My dad tosses a Frisbee to Alex. Alex dives for the Frisbee and misses.

"Why don't you get a drink?" Dad says to me. He sips beer from his travel mug. He nods toward the swim-up bar along the far side of the pool. It's busy with sunbaked adults. "You can get something with alcohol if you want. They won't ask you how old you are."

"I don't drink," I lie. I got wasted with Jamy in her basement a few nights ago before I left with my family for Cuba. We drank her parents' beers. She'll turn nineteen before I do.

The sun roasts my pink shoulders. I itch behind my neck with pruned fingers and short, bitten nails.

"Did you put sunscreen on?" Dad asks me.

"Yes." I haven't.

"Put more on. You're already going red. It's the first day."

"I'm fine," I say. "I don't get burnt."

"Alex, you too. Your face is red. Go get some from Mom." My sister's face, framed by loose light brown ringlets, is red.

"No, I want a tan." She disappears under the water.

I scratch at the itch on my shoulder.

I stare in the mirror. My face is red. My shoulders are redder.

I press my index finger onto my shoulder and lift after a second. A hot white circle the size of my fingertip glows against the sunburn and then fades back to red again. I scratch my shoulders and down my arms, leaving fine trails of torn skin behind.

At breakfast, Mom notices my itching. "You're putting on sunscreen today," she says. Her skin is a dark brown. My dad is darker. *How come everyone in this family tans so well except for me?*

I tear off the end of a croissant and pop the fluffy piece of bread into my mouth. I chew. I try not to itch.

I shake my legs. My hands tremble, shaking the copy of *The Girl with the Dragon Tattoo*. The words dance around. The edges of the pages are damp under my sweaty hands.

Mom looks over from her patio chair. "Jump in the pool," she says. "Maybe it'll feel good on your itchy burns."

"My burns aren't itchy," I say.

She presses her mouth into a hard line. "Hmm." She turns away. Her sunglasses catch the glare of the sun.

I inch my chair deeper into the shade of the large umbrella, away from the sunlight. It's like a game. Every ten minutes, the shade shifts, and so does my chair.

I dig sunscreen out of the mess of bunched towels, books and bottles of lotion in my mom's bag. I slap sunscreen onto my arms first. My pores absorb the lotion. The itching subsides. *Success!* I pour more into my hands and spread it across my skin. Relief on my chest, on my stomach, on my back. My arms are itchy again. I squeeze more. I paint myself with sunscreen.

"Enough of that," my mom says. "You need to rub all that in now, you look silly."

"This helps!" I smear more sunscreen on my back. "I can't stop itching."

"Stop itching and you won't itch."

"I *can't*." My skin feels like it's bubbling. I clamp my eyes shut and breathe in deeply. *Don't itch,* I start telling myself. *Don't itch. Don't itch. Don't itch.*

I clench my fists and spring up from my patio chair. *The Girl with the Dragon Tattoo* tumbles into a puddle of water by my feet. The pages soak up the moisture like my skin with the sunscreen.

I jog to the pool and slip on the patio. I drop into the water. Clouds of sunscreen float off of my skin and fade into the water. I shut my eyes and lay back. "That feels good," I say to nobody.

The relief in the water lasts for five minutes.

When I scratch the back of my neck, I draw blood.

At night, I don't sleep.

"Don't itch at the table," Dad says.

"I wasn't itching," I whimper. I scratch my leg one more time.

"He's itching," Alex says.

"*Die.*"

I pick up my fork, stab a piece of chicken, and throw it into my mouth. I stab another piece. The itching in my arms fires up. I drop the fork. It clangs against my plate. I itch.

"*Mathew,*" Mom hisses.

"I'm not making this up!" I say. "I itch all over! I didn't sleep last night, Mom! I'm so tired!" I slam my head against the table and itch my arms. When I was a kid, my parents never believed me when I told them I was sick. They said I'm overdramatic. They still say I'm overdramatic.

"Well, what could it be?"

"I don't *know,*" I say. "I itch really bad when I'm in bed. Or when I towel off after my shower. It's worst then."

Mom looks at Dad. "Maybe he's allergic to something."

79

"*Yes*," I say. "Do you have any medicine?"

She rummages around in her bag. "I didn't bring any antihistamines," she says.

"I need to see a doctor."

"Enough," says Dad.

"John, he could be allergic to something," says Mom. "With his luck our son will die."

Alex laughs.

"This is not funny," I say. "Remember when you cried for three days because you thought there was sand in your eye?"

"There *was*," she hisses.

"And *I'm* itchy! Stop being so sassy!"

"*Enough*," says Dad.

Mom stands from the table. "Okay. Let's see if the gift shop has anything. They might have medicine, or maybe cooling lotion. We'll look for something."

I follow Mom into the resort lobby. Sunlight shines through large open squares in the ceiling above us, and birds rush by our heads, flying between the columns around the perimeter of the lobby in the place of walls. We pass other vacationers, bloated and brown from their leisure. I try my hardest not to lift the back of my shirt and scratch the top of my butt as we walk past girls who look like they're my age.

Mom points to the gift shop past the reception desk.

She pulls the glass door open. The door chimes. The shop is crammed with stacks of t-shirts and glassware and post-cards, all decorated with the Cuban flag. Mom asks the woman behind the desk if she has any allergy medicine. She doesn't, she says in broken English, but she pulls out a map of the resort like the ones my family was given when we checked in a few days ago. She pokes a small building near the top corner with a brown finger. The number 26 sits above the building in a circle. The legend says that it's an on site doctor's office. "That looks far," I say to Mom.

Outside the shop, Mom asks the people working at the reception counter about how to get to the medical building. I wait on the couch. I scratch my ankle.

She walks toward me holding her map. The warm breeze catches her long sundress and her long curly hair. "We can't walk there," she says to me. "We're going to take one of their carts." She crosses the lobby and flags down a man in an orange shirt at the wheel of a cart with three rows of empty seats.

"We're going here," she says, pointing to the doctor's office on the map. When the driver protests, she slips him a few American dollar bills.

The cart trips over the rocks in the road. Each bump hurts my back. I bring my feet up to my seat, hug my legs against my body, and rest my chin on my knees. I scratch my legs.

"We're gonna die out here," I tell Mom. The familiar buildings of the resort disappear behind tall palm trees and dense green shrubs. "We're gonna get mugged, and then kidnapped, and then sold for parts."

"No we will not."

"I just want to live long enough to see the next Batman movie."

Mom passes me her travel mug. I take a large swig of warm water, expecting it to be beer.

"If this doctor doesn't help," I say, "I'm going to kill myself."

"Don't say that," she hisses.

Our driver pulls up to the small building on the edge of the resort. Mom thanks the man and passes him a few more paper bills.

We step through an entryway without a door. The small room is white and sparse, aside from a glass table and two chairs. A woman smiles from behind a glass counter and asks us what we're looking for. Bugs crawl across the wall behind her.

"I think my son is allergic to something," Mom says. "We think it's the detergent used on the sheets and towels. We just need antihistamines."

"You need to see the doctor?" the woman says slowly.

"No, we just need medicine. Pills."

"You need to see the doctor."

I look at my mom and frown.

We follow the woman through a door into a second room, smaller than the first. I sit atop a doctor's chair. The wall across from me is lined with overflowing medicine cabinets. "She will be here soon," the receptionist woman says.

Fifteen minutes pass. "There's one thing this place has in common with Canada," I say to my mom.

"What's that?"

"You always have to wait a long time to see a doctor."

"Yup." Mom crosses her arms. "When she comes in, we're going to say that all we want is medicine, not a checkup. I don't want any crazy bills."

I scratch my back.

The door swings open and a woman with long dark hair and a clipboard enters the room. "What is the problem?" she asks with only a hint of a Cuban accent.

"I'm allergic to something," I say. "I can't stop itching."

"We just need some allergy medicine," my mom says.

"I see," the doctor says.

Silence hangs over the room for a minute.

"Just allergy medicine," my mom repeats.

The doctor nods.

"You can buy some at the counter," she says finally. "You didn't need to see me." She smiles and disappears through the door.

"*Waste of time,*" I mutter under my breath. Mom pushes through the door. I take my time climbing off of the chair to follow her back into the reception area. I itch freely.

I meet Mom in the waiting room. The woman at the counter hands her a sheet of six pills, and in exchange Mom gives her a wad of cash. She turns from the counter, frowns, and steps outside into the sunlight. I join her in the heat. She pops a pill into my hand.

"It's not going to work immediately," she says.

I place the pill on my tongue and swallow hard. I force the dry pill down my throat. I shut my eyes and itch my shoulders.

LIVER

I press the inside of my arm against my nose. The fridge emits an awful odor. My roommate's bowl of unfinished salsa sits uncovered on the bottom shelf. When I poured myself a glass of milk a few days ago, I smelled the carton and it smelled like tomatoes and onions. "You have to put saran wrap over something like that," I told her. She said she would. She didn't. After all, this is the same roommate who left raw chicken in the fridge for three weeks until it turned green, because she figured it didn't need to be frozen.

I pinch my nose with my left thumb and forefinger and reach my right hand deep into the fridge. I knock a carton of eggs into a half eaten loaf of bread and I wrap my fingers around the cold neck of a bottle of Canadian.

I shut the fridge behind me. My roommate Sam and our friends Nick and Daria laugh from the living room. "We need help with the puzzle!" Sam calls. Sam has recently taken up jigsaw puzzles as a hobby. When she finishes, she tapes the back of the puzzle together with masking tape, and hangs the plaque on our blank residence walls. I look through the doorway to the kitchen at the unicorn taped against the wall and frown.

I join my friends in the living room. Daria and Nick hold a large piece of cardboard under the edge of the table while Sam slowly inches the completed puzzle—a purple fairy against a moon—toward the cardboard. "We need more hands!" Daria laughs. I twist the cap off of my Canadian, drop the cap into my pocket, and approach the table.

Sam stops. "You're having another one?" She narrows her eyes and raises her right eyebrow.

"Uh – yeah?"

"Hmm."

Sam, Daria, Nick and I had gone out for dinner to Swiss Chalet on a whim. Daria drove. I had a beer with dinner.

"Sam," I say, "I'm having a beer. I already had one. I think I'll be okay."

"Okay," she says. "I'm just concerned about your drinking."

"What?"

"I said I'm concerned about your drinking habits."

"Are you saying I have a problem?" My cheeks flush. I clamp onto the beer harder. Beads of sweat run down the glass and pool against my tightly wrapped hand.

Sam frowns. "Don't put words in my mouth."

I raise the top of the bottle, tilt it against my open mouth, and drink. The cool beer bubbles in my mouth. "*Ahhhh*," I say. "Well, if I had a drinking problem, you'd know it."

I set the bottle down on the low coffee table and grab the roll of masking tape. "How can I help?" I ask.

"We've got this," Sam says flatly.

I shrug. "If you say so. Maybe this one can go in your room, instead of out here."

I turn from the table, wave goodbye to Daria and Nick, and push open the door to my bedroom with my shoulder. I twist the deadbolt behind me. I drop down onto my bed, open my MacBook with my free hand, and lay back against the two black pillows stacked against the headboard. I open a new browser and drink the rest of my beer.

I push the end of the red streamer against the top of the wall with my left hand and slap a long piece of tape across it with my right. The streamer sticks. I unravel the roll and step back from the wall, pulling the streamer tight. I spin on the spot, step up onto the coffee table, and attach the streamer to one of the ceiling fan. blades I secure it to the dusty blade with more tape, and then rip the rest of the roll with my fingers after where I taped it down. The streamer hangs from the wall to the ceiling fan with a soft droop. *Success. Four more to go.*

"Did you get balloons?" Sam calls from her bedroom.

"No," I answer. "Just streamers."

"Hmm."

"If you wanted balloons you should have bought your own decorations. It's *your* party."

"*Hmm.*"

I step down from the table. I bunch up the sleeve of my sweater and wipe the sweaty footprints I left behind on the table.

Sam and I had gotten into an argument earlier over her birthday. It started when she found out that I invited Katherine, our next door neighbour. Katherine lived on the same floor as everyone in first year, and was Daria's roommate. I figured everyone would want to see her. Sam told me she only wanted her closest friends around, and she wouldn't listen to me when I said that adding one more person to the small party of five would be okay. I left her alone to stir in her anger.

A few hours after that, I asked her if we were still going

to be drinking. She told me she didn't feel like it, and would rather sit around without alcohol instead. I told her I had been looking forward to a night of drinking all week, which caused her to explode at me. "You can have fun without alcohol, Matt," she kept saying. "It hurts me that you don't care about celebrating my birthday, and that you only care about drinking."

"I don't," I said. "I'm just upset because I'm a bit disappointed."

She told me then that I had a drinking problem.

I tape a streamer to the last of the ceiling fan blades. I step down from the table for the last time, ball my fists against my hips, and admire my work. The five strands of red paper flare out from the ceiling fan at five points, making our sparse residence unit look like the inside of a circus tent. I turn to the curtain of streamers I taped in across the entryway to the main room. "Not bad," I say aloud.

Heels click against the hardwood floor. Sam passes through the curtain of streamers. Her thick legs are squeezed into tight black leggings. A blazer with studs on the shoulders stretches across her broad chest and stomach. Her wiry black hair is pulled up into a messy bunch on the top of her head, fastened by a cheap-looking blue flower clip. Dark black makeup circles her eyes and blends in with her dark brown skin.

"This looks nice," she says.

"We aren't going anywhere tonight," I say, pointing at her heels. "We're staying in and not drinking, remember?" I look down at my sweatpants.

She crosses her arms over her stomach and glares. "The room could use more streamers," she says. She turns back through the curtain and disappears into her room.

I rip a small piece of streamer and tape it on the wall beside the jigsaw puzzle of the purple fairy and moon. The streamer hangs limp. *There.*

Daria, Nick and Steven arrive a little bit after eight. Sam greets each of them with a big hug. I lean back into the low cushioned chair and wave. Our friends take seats around the coffee table. Sam grabs my black digital camera and takes candid pictures of everyone as we open and start a game of Monopoly. I keep out of the conversation. I lean forward only to throw the dice across the board. Sam sighs as the die crash into one of the game pieces and messes up the pile of Chance cards in the middle. I move my piece. I toss Monopoly money onto the board. "I'll buy the railroad," I say.

Knock knock knock. I jump up from my seat. I push streamers out of my way. I open the front door and welcome Katherine inside. She pushes her long dirty blonde hair over her ear with her hand and kicks her brown winter boots off with her heels. "Party's barely started," I whisper to her. She follows me back into the room.

"Happy Birthday, Sam," she says. She hands Sam a card and a small box wrapped in paper.

"Oh," Sam says. "You shouldn't have bought me anything."

"It's your birthday, of course I bought you something."

Katherine takes a seat on the floor beside my chair. She pulls a bottle of white wine out of the purse slung across her shoulder. She sets the bottle down on the table beside the game of Monopoly.

"Is nobody drinking?" she says, looking around the room.

Sam glares.

"No," I say. "I'm drinking. I'll get you a glass."

I enter the kitchen and grab a wine glass from the cupboard. I hold the glass up to my eye and inspect it. No specks of dirt, no marks. *Clean enough.*

I reach into the freezer and pull out the forty of Captain Morgan's Dark Rum my grandfather gave to me when I moved onto residence. Specks of ice sting my palm. I grab a can of Coke Zero from the fridge and find a clean glass. I juggle the glasses in my right hand and the drinks in my left.

I slam the forty of rum onto the table beside Katherine's bottle of wine. I hand her the wine glass. "For you." She snaps the seal of her bottle and twists off the cap. I pour my glass halfway full with rum, dig my finger under the tab on the Coke can, and top off the rest of my glass with the dark crackling pop.

The alcohol burns the cracks of my lips and burns my throat when I swallow. Sam stares at her nails.

We continue the game. I finish my drink. I pour more rum into my cup and set the bottle back down into its ring of water on the wooden table. Katherine finishes a second glass of wine.

"Hey, Matt."

I turn to Nick.

"Would it… would it be okay if I had some of your rum?"

Usually, I hate sharing my alcohol. "You bet," I say.

"Could I have some, too?" asks Steven.

"You know what would be fun?" Daria starts. "Shots. You have shot glasses, right Sam?"

"Yes," Sam mumbles.

I collect clean cups and shot glasses from the kitchen and set them out in a line alongside the game of Monopoly. "You're lucky I'm feeling generous," I say, unscrewing the cap on my bottle of rum. I splash more rum into my drink before I pass the bottle to Daria. I take a long drink of straight rum.

Daria pours rum into the line of shot glasses. It splashes against the table and the game of Monopoly. The alcohol stains the corner of a Monopoly bill. I take one of the full glasses. It shakes in my hand. The surface of the alcohol dances against the glass rim. Daria hands out the rest of the shot glasses.

I pass one to Katherine. I hold the shot glass in front of my face. "To Sam," I say loudly. My cheeks burn red. My head buzzes. "Happy 20th Birthday."

The room chimes into a "Happy Birthday!" in unison.

I knock the shot back. The alcohol stings. I smile. Sam frowns.

BLADDER

"Mathew, do you need to use the washroom?"

"No."

"Are you sure?"

"*Yes*, I'm sure."

Mom shakes her head. "John, try to get him to go to the washroom," she says to Dad.

Dad shrugs. "He says he doesn't have to go."

"Will you drink some water, then? It's hot and you haven't had any yet." Mom holds out a plastic water bottle. I push it away.

"I'm not thirsty. I want to go on the Tower of Terror!"

Mom throws her hands up. "Alright, fine. But don't tell

me you're thirsty in ten minutes, okay?"

"Mother," I say. I ball my fists and press them against my hips. "I'm nine. I know when I'm thirsty. I'm like a camel. Camels retain water, didn't you know? I'm like a camel. Can we *please* go on the Tower of Terror now?"

A tall brown hotel towers high into the overcast sky. Cracks spread across the walls. Dusts smears across the windows stacked in vertical columns up the face of the building. Spikes shoot out of the peaks on the shingled roof. A huge flickering fluorescent sign that reads "The Hollywood Tower Hotel" sits across the width of the building. Beneath the sign, at the top of each column of windows, sits a set of closed shutters. *Bang!* The shutters fly open. An elevator cart full of screaming people pops up into the open window, floats, then falls out of view. The shudders slam shut. The screaming fades.

I grin at Mom and Dad. "I'm so excited!"

When Mom and Dad told me we were going to Disney World, I decided the first ride I wanted to go on was the Tower of Terror at MGM Studios. "It's like the Drop Zone at Wonderland!" I told them. "You sit in an elevator cart, and then they bring you up to the top, and then *whoosh*, you drop back down!" We have a Disney World promotional video at home. We got it when my parents booked the tickets. My favourite part is the scene about the Tower of Terror. I've watched it twenty times.

"Is Alex coming, too?" I ask Mom.

My sister shakes her head. Her curly light brown hair bounces from under the Mickey Mouse ears on her head. She buries her face into the denim of Mom's jeans. "I don't want to go on it," she says.

"You're a baby," I tell her. She sticks her tongue out at me.

"She should be okay," Dad says to Mom. "It can't be worse than the alien ride."

The first ride my parents took us on at the Magic Kingdom was a ride where an alien breaks out of its display and attacks the people sitting in the audience in darkness. Alex cried for hours, and I was too afraid to go on anything else.

Dad holds his hand out to Alex. "Come on, it'll be fun," he says. Alex takes his hand. Dad leads the way.

We pass under a big arch beside the building. A sign beside the arch reads "*Wait time: sixty minutes from this point.*"

I frown at Dad. "We don't have to wait that long, do we?"

He shrugs. "Be patient. It might be a little while."

We walk down a stone path and join the line of people behind a couple of teenagers in torn denim shorts and cool looking sunglasses. The line stretches far ahead of them into a mess of overgrown ferns and bushes. I bounce up and down on my heels. "I hate waiting."

A mosquito pricks my neck. I smack it. The sunburn on the back of my neck stings.

Mom pulls a bottle of sunscreen out of her leather backpack. She squirts lotion onto her palm and slaps it onto the back of my neck. "You didn't put any on, did you?"

"*Stop*," I say. "I can do it myself." I push her hand. I rub sunscreen onto my skin. I accidentally get sunscreen on the collar of my black Mickey Mouse t-shirt.

"You're getting burnt," Dad says. "Why don't you wear a hat like we tell you?"

"Because I don't like hats." I pat my curly hair, cross my arms, and turn away from my parents.

"Well, you're going to start listening to us. You're going to use the washroom when we're done with the ride. Alright?"

"Fine," I say, "but I won't have to go."

A small pressure flashes just under my stomach. *I don't need to pee*, I tell myself.

We shuffle forward into the shadow of the building. I climb onto the metal bars dividing the line and look above the heads of the people in front of us. The line zigzags back and forth between stone pillars, under trellis roofs, and through tangles of vines. Every so often the shutters fly open on the front of the building. Screams fill the air for just a second, and then the silence takes over again.

"Are we there yet?" asks Alex.

After what seems like forever, we pass through a set of wooden doors and into a large hotel lobby. The lobby looks deserted. Cracks run across the plaster on the walls over patterned wallpaper. A statue of an eagle with cobwebs stretched between its open wings stands in the middle of the room on top of an expensive looking wooden table. Leather peels up from the cushions on the couch and armchairs. Behind the eagle sits a tall fireplace. The ceiling is even taller than the fireplace and is covered in great wooden beams. I look straight up to the chandelier above me. The dirty crystals are covered in more cobwebs. "This is so *cool*," I whisper.

A reception desk lines the far wall, but there's nobody working. We follow the line forward through the lobby. I pass an armchair and reach under the red velvet rope of the line and stick my finger into the cobwebs caught on the chair's legs. "Don't do that," Mom hisses. I pull my hand back. The tip of my finger is covered in dust, and a cobweb is caught in the jagged edge of my bitten fingernail.

"The dust is *real*," I whisper to my sister.

The chandelier shakes. I jump. The pressure under my stomach returns. It feels heavier.

My sister screams when the chandelier shakes again. "I don't want to go on this ride," she cries. "I'm scared, Mommy." Alex reaches for Mom to pick her up. Her cries bounce against the ceiling. The teens in front of us turn and look at my screaming sister. I look down.

"I'm going to step out of line with her," Mom says to Dad. "We'll wait for you by the exit, okay?" She takes my sister's hand and turns back the way we came. They skirt around the people behind us and disappear into the bushes.

"I *told* you she's a baby," I say to Dad.

Dad holds a finger up to his lips.

Dad and I follow the line past the front desk and through a door to what looks like the hotel's basement. The room we enter looks like Freddy Krueger's boiler room in *A Nightmare on Elm Street*. The line of people in front of us folds back and forth again through a maze of rusted pipes. Steam blows overheard and the copper pipes along the ceiling rattle against one another. On the furthest side of the room, I can see a line of elevator doors. *That must be where the ride picks you up.*

The pressure under my stomach hurts. The pipes near my head shake. The thought of water makes me feel like I need to pee even worse. I cross my legs and sway on my feet. *Almost there. Almost there.*

"Do you have to use the washroom?" Dad asks me.

"Nope."

He narrows his eyes. "Hm. Okay. If you say so."

I squeeze my legs together to stop the pressure. I shut my eyes and twist my face. "Okay," I say, the words jumping from my mouth. "I really need to pee. I have to go."

"You should've gone when your mother asked you!"

"Can we get out of line and just come back? They'd let us do that, right?"

"We've waited for close to an hour now. Wait a few minutes more." Dad frowns. "Maybe you won't need to go as bad when you sit down on the ride."

I squeeze harder. *Think about anything else.* The pressure grows. I moan. There's nothing I can do.

Warm liquid runs down my legs and stains my jeans a dark blue. It puddles around my sneakers. It runs down the slope of the floor, winding through the maze of grout between the brown tiles. It slides down around the teenagers' feet. They look down in shock, then at my face, and then at my jeans. They break into laughter, and I hear the people in front of them say, "Look, that kid pissed his pants." I shut my eyes and pretend nobody can see me. Dad clamps his hand on my shoulder.

The pressure is gone.

The teenagers laugh.

The line inches forward. My jeans slosh as I walk.

"Your mother and I told you to go to the washroom," Dad hisses.

"I didn't have to then."

"Did you get scared?"

"I'm *not* scared!" My face reddens.

A man dressed like a bellhop ushers people onto the middle elevator. The teens in front of us board the ride. The bellhop extends a velvet rope across the line in front of me and my dad. "You're on the next one," he says. He looks down at my jeans. "Is someone scared of the ride?" he snickers.

"*No*," I say.

My dad steps in front of me and blocks my jeans with his body. "He's fine," he says.

"Just don't get any on the seat," says the bellhop.

The elevator on the far right opens with a *ding*. The man unlatches the velvet rope. Dad pushes me lightly. I slosh forward. I pass through an open gate onto a wide elevator cart filled with three rows of black seats. "Take a seat in the back," Dad whispers. I climb the steps in the middle of the aisle, turn into the last row, and sit in the back corner. Dad sits down in the seat beside me.

I grab the seatbelt and pull it across my waist. *Click*. The buckle rests on my damp lap. I shrink in my seat. The plastic seat squeaks.

The ride fills with the people in line behind us. I keep my eyes shut. "Everyone on?" the bellhop asks. "Buckle up." He shuts the gate across the entryway and the elevator doors close. My heart races. A light inside of the cart flickers. A gear screeches and the elevator card leaps up.

As we rise, my stomach sinks.

I squeeze my legs together. I'm scared. I have to pee again.

LEG

The car screeches when Olivia throws it into park. "Shh, Fat Betty," she says. She pulls the key out of the ignition and the squealing car rests. We call her car Fat Betty because it barely accelerates anymore.

Olivia unclicks her seatbelt and pushes her Ray Bans over to her forehead "Are you ready for this?"

I gulp. "Yup."

I stare through Fat Betty's windshield. A woman with a red bandana, aviator sunglasses, and sleeves of tattoos inked down of her both arms sits on a bench in front of the tattoo parlour and smokes a cigarette. A sign above the glass shop front reads "Anchor's Tattoo and Piercing" in cursive letters made of cartoon ropes. Anchors sit on either side of the shop's name.

I groan.

"What?" Olivia asks.

"Nothing. It's just real now, you know?" My heart thumps against the seatbelt pulled tight across my chest. "I mean, yeah, I put the money down on the appointment and everything, but now we're here, and this is actually happening, and I can't change my mind. You know? I don't know." The fabric of my plain black t-shirt, bunched up high in my armpits, is warm with sweat.

"Get excited!" Olivia flashes a grin. She opens her door and steps out of the car.

I climb out of Fat Betty, slam the heavy silver door behind me, and follow Olivia through the front door of the shop. The guy at the counter looks up when we walk in. I remember him from when I booked my appointment a week ago. I was surprised to find out he has tattoos. There aren't any on on his bare arms or legs. From behind his thick framed glasses, he looks like a bit of a nerd.

"I have an appointment," I say.

"Right," he says. "Name?"

I tell him.

"Amanda is almost through with her break"—he points at the window behind me to the woman on the bench— "so you both can have a seat"—he points at the leather couch in front of the window —"and she'll be with you soon."

I sink into the couch. My sweaty legs squeak against the black leather. Olivia sits a chair beside the couch. She reaches for a pile of magazines sitting on top of the glass coffee table in front of us and grabs the magazine from the top of the stack. She points at a woman, naked except for her tattoos, sitting on top of a motorcycle. "What do you think," she says. "I'm going to do this."

"Please don't."

She laughs, leans back into her chair, and flips through the magazine.

The tattoo parlour is empty, except for me, Olivia, and the nerdy guy at the counter. Dark hardwood lines the floors. The seafoam green walls are covered in framed photographs of art inked on both paper and skin. A couple of floor length mirrors, framed with collections of Polaroids and sketches on torn pieces of lined paper, stand along the walls. A folded table sits against the wall behind the counter.

The back corner of the shop looks like a doctor's office. Sterile white tiles on the walls, tall medicine cabinets with frosted glass doors, and lines of tools above a sink surround a white dentist's chair. A limp curtain hangs bunched against the far wall. The track runs around the corner of the shop along the popcorn ceiling.

I let out a deep breath.

"Don't be nervous," Olivia says.

"I'm not nervous."

"Well, you look it."

"I'm afraid it's going to hurt." I spot a needle kit on a rolling tray behind the front counter.

"It's doesn't hurt that bad."

"*That* bad?"

"Well, it *is* a needle. At least you're getting it done where there's a lot of flesh. Mine hurt." Cursive black writing stretches out in a line across the top of Olivia's foot. It peeks out from under the leather straps of her sandals.

The bell above the door chimes and Amanda enters the shop. "You're my appointment?" she says. She extends her hand to me. I shake it. She smells like cigarette smoke and mint.

"Nice to meet you."

"So what are we doing today?"

"I, uh, want to get a tattoo on the back of my leg. My right leg." I pull my red iPod Touch out of the pocket of my charcoal gray shorts. I swipe my finger across the lock screen and leave behind a streak of sweat on the surface. I poke at the icons and find the picture I saved to the device last night. "That's what I want." I show Amanda the symbol.

"I've seen that before."

"It's, uh, from *Harry Potter*," I say quietly.

"Cool. So first, let's figure out a size. How big are you thinking?"

"Whatever looks best."

"Okay. I'll print it off like a temporary tattoo, and we'll place it on the back of your leg to see if you like the size and the position. Does that make sense?"

I nod.

"Give me a few minutes." Amanda skirts around the front counter, leans over the shoulder of the reception guy, and slams her fingers onto the keys of the computer. I sent a file of the image to the email account written on the back of the business card I took when I booked my appointment last Saturday. I picked the best looking image off of Google.

The printer hums. "You can come back here," Amanda says. She grabs the folded table from against the wall, unfolds its legs, and snaps it into place in the middle of the floor. It looks like a massage table. I approach it. Olivia follows.

"Are you getting something done, too?" Amanda asks Olivia.

"Oh, no," she says. "I'm just here for support." She takes a seat in a foldout chair beside the mirror.

I lift my leg to climb on top of the table. "Not yet," Amanda says. She holds a pink disposable razor in front of her face. "Turn around."

My sandals squeak when I turn on the spot. Amanda kneels on the ground behind me. She scrapes the razor down the back of my leg. It stings.

"Oh my god, Matt," Olivia laughs. "That's so gross."

"I can't help that I have hair on my legs," I say. "I'm sorry."

"It's fine," Amanda says. "I've dealt with worse."

She drags the blade in quick swipes. When she finishes, she flashes me the front of the blade and laughs. Bunches of hair stick between the strips of metal. She tosses the razor into a garbage bin beside the front counter. I look over my shoulder. A square bald patch of skin pops out amidst the hair.

"That's so awkward looking," Olivia says. She laughs again.

"Shut up."

Amanda grabs the glossy sheet of paper from the printer and kneels behind me again. "This is like those temporary tattoos you'd get as a kid," she says, holding the paper against my leg. The cool surface of the paper stings my newly shaved skin. She places her palm against the back of the paper and holds pressure for a minute. "Let's see," she says, peeling the now blank paper from my leg.

I walk up to the mirror beside Olivia, turn, and look over my shoulder. A perfect triangle with a circle inside of it and a line down the middle stands on my skin in thick navy blue lines. "What's it mean?" Amanda says.

"It's the Deathly Hallows symbol, from the last *Harry Potter* book. I'm a huge fan." I stare at the temporary stamp in the mirror. "It looks perfect."

Amanda claps her hand. "Well then, it's time. Get up on the table, if you would."

Olivia smiles at me. I climb onto the table on my stomach. My feet hang over the end of the table and my sandals slip off and crash to the floor. Amanda sits on a stool and wheels herself near my right leg. She drags the rolling tray with the needle kit and ink with her.

"I'm going to trace over the temporary tattoo like a guide," she says.

"Mhmm." I gulp.

"First tattoo?"

"What gave it away?"

She laughs. "You'll get used to the pain."

She dips the needle into a pot of black ink and flicks a switch. The needle springs to life. *Buzzzzzzzz.* "I'm starting with the outline," she says.

I shut my eyes. I breathe in.

The tip of the needle pokes into my skin like a splinter. She presses down on the needle, down into my flesh, and I wince at the pain. The buzzing needle inches across my skin like a searing blade. I picture my skin splitting apart. My stomach sinks.

And then the buzzing stops, and the tip of the needle is lifted from my calf. I exhale.

"Not so bad, huh?" says Amanda.

I look at Olivia and pout. "It's manageable, right?" she says.

"Absolutely," I lie.

I turn my head and press my ear and cheek against the hard surface of the table. I stare at my reflection in the mirror beside me.

"Focus on something," Olivia says. I pick her iPhone, sitting in her lap, dressed in a case that looks like a Pokéball from *Pokémon*.

"How much did you cover?" I ask Amanda.

She gives a big laugh. "That was, like, a millimeter. This will probably take an hour and a bit." *Buzzzzzzzzz.* "Ready for more?"

"Alright."

I shut my eyes. I breathe in.

The cold tip of the needle meets my skin again.

Buzz.

Sear.

Slice.

Stop.

Rest.

Repeat.

FOOT

I press the can of Pabst Blue Ribbon against my lips and take a long drink of warm beer. It's my seventh. Or eighth. Or ninth.

"Are you excited for your trip?"

Sarah's blue eyes meet mine. The alcohol in my system makes my vision funny. Her head is a big blur of dyed crimson hair.

"Super excited," I say over the music. The speakers on the shelf above my head pump out the beat of a song. A Brockhouse party rule is nobody messes with the playlist. The iPod is shattered and unresponsive to touch, and Neil has hidden the remote for the dock so that nobody can change the song. To make things democratic, everyone requested a bunch of songs each. I smile to myself whenever Lady Gaga comes on.

"I'm so jealous of you," Sarah says. She takes a drink from a bottle of Canadian. "I want to go to Florida."

"You should be jealous," I slur. "I'm going to Hogwarts." My family's summer trip this year is to Orlando. We're renting a house, and we're visiting Disney World and the Wizarding World of Harry Potter at Universal Studios. I've been saving money to buy a wand. Our flight leaves in a week.

I finish my beer and crush the can in my hand. "I need to pee," I announce. I climb to my feet. "Be back," I tell Sarah. "Save my seat."

I squeeze between people dancing in the middle of the room. I edge around a game of beer pong at the dining room table and pat my friend Neil on the shoulder as he sinks a ping-pong ball into one of Amy's cups. "Damn!" she yells. She pulls the wet ball out of her cup, presses the cup to her lips, and chugs. I reach up to the shelf that runs around the perimeter of the room. My can finds a home between an empty bottle of Girl's Night Out wine and an empty jar labeled "Amy's Car Fund."

I wander into the narrow kitchen jump into the background of the picture Steph K is taking on her iPhone of Janeen and the other Steph, Steph Popoff. "Hey!" they yell, pointing at me.

"Pick a nice filter on Instagram," I tell Steph as I squeeze between her and the counter.

I'm drunk, but I know my way around Brockhouse pretty well. Brockhouse is the bungalow where my best friend Amy and her roommates Lauren, Neil, and the two Stephs live during the school year, ten minutes away from Brock University. I've been close friends with Amy since grade one, and we went to high school with the Stephs and Neil. Amy knew Lauren through hockey.

The washroom on the main floor is at the end of the hall between Amy and Lauren's bedrooms. I pass beside the fridge covered in magnets, grocery lists, and Internet memes. Facing out from the kitchen, the washroom is directly in front of me at the end of the narrow hall.

Boxes marked "Steph Popoff's Stuff" litter the floor. Popoff's parents are moving back to the Bahamas permanently, she told me earlier, so she's moving some of her stuff into the new apartment she's sharing with her sister in Burlington. Piles of textbooks with cracked spines, heaps of clothes in a spectrum of colour, and pairs of mismatched shoes cover the floor not occupied by boxes. My foot slips on a sweater, and I accidentally kick a lamp.

The closed washroom door stands like a brick wall in front of me. I slump to the right against Amy's bedroom door. The door swings open under my weight and I stumble forward into her room. The Christmas lights around the window cast a colourful glow across my face. The light reflects off a wall covered in printed pictures of family and friends. I spot my face in the display of pictures.

The song in the main room fades to a close and the roars of conversation and laughter rise over the moment of silence. A new beat thumps. recognize the beat instantly. "212" by Azealia Banks. Mine and Amy's unofficial song. We know every word.

I have sixteen counts to find Amy before the rapping starts.

Amy screams my name from the main room. I run. I wobble around the boxes. I jump. My left foot catches on the corner of a box of shoes. I crash down with all of my weight on my right foot. My ankle twists and my entire body presses down on the outermost bone of my foot. *Crack*. I feel it snap. I falter. I throw my hands against the walls for balance. I lift my left foot and shout when my weight transfers onto my right. Pain explodes up my shin. I throw myself toward the entryway to the main room and lean my shoulder against the wall, catching the corner of a *Grey's Anatomy* poster under the weight of my body.

The first verse of "212" begins.

Amy sees me through a break in the crowd of people. She sprints toward me. Her flushed cheeks match the red stripes on her shirt. She shouts the lyrics in my face. I force a smile.

She gasps for breath between two lines and spills her beer on the ground. She swipes her sock across the small spill and notices my foot. "Are you alright?" she asks me.

"I… no," I say. My head feels light. I remember to breathe. "I think I fucked up my foot." I look down.

My foot has swollen to the size of a melon. The skin is as red as Amy's face. I balance on my left foot and try to lift my swollen foot up to my waist without falling over. I prod the swelling with my finger. My finger shoots pain into my skin like a bullet. I feel a small hard piece of something floating amidst the swollen mass. I slide down the wall, dizzy from the pain and from the alcohol.

Steph K wraps her arm around my back. "Let's get you downstairs to your futon," she says.

She guides me through the kitchen. I wave at Lauren and Nick. They back away to make room for Steph and I to pass and make faces when they notice my foot. "Nothing but a scratch," I slur, trying to make myself laugh. I flash a thumbs-up at them.

"212" draws to a close.

I pause at the top of the stairs to the basement and look at Steph. My head rolls. I try to focus my vision on her face, on her blue eyes, on the freckles on her nose. "I can't make it down those stairs," I say.

"Yes you can," she says. "Then we'll get you another beer."

"I do need that."

I grip the walls. My hands slip, slick with sweat. I shift my weight onto my left foot and slowly place my right onto the first step down. The bottom of my foot meets cool linoleum and the pain explodes at the light touch. I inhale sharply and lift my left foot. "*Fuck!*" I scream when I transfer all of my weight onto my swollen foot, and I quickly drop my left foot onto the next step. I take heavy breaths. "Piece of cake," I say. When I reach the landing halfway down the stairs, tears stream down my face.

I take one last step onto the hardwood floor of the basement. I duck my head against the low ceiling. The futon a few feet away from me jumps around in my vision, and the many pairs of eyes in the collage of Natalie Portman taped to the wall above the futon stare me down. I jump at the futon and crash into my backpack and a pile of pillows and blankets. I flip myself over and prop myself against the wall. I sandwich a pillow between my back and Natalie Portman's Chanel ad. My swollen foot rests atop the metal bar at the opposite end of the futon. It throbs pain in unison with my pulse. "I could use that beer," I tell Steph.

"That looks awful," she says. She grabs another pillow. I lift my leg and she places it under my foot. The feathery pillow cradles my swollen melon of a foot.

Footsteps patter down the stairs. Amy's blonde hair

and Sarah's red hair at the bottom of the stairs are blurry blots in my vision. "Yikes," Amy says.

She places a can of Pabst in front of my face. I snatch the can, lift the tab, and chug.

Sarah sits on the edge of the futon. "Are you alright?" she asks.

"I want to die."

She hands me an ice filled Ziploc and a dishtowel. I press the plastic bag against the swelling. The cold stings. "Mother of God," I say. I take the towel and wrap it around the bag of ice to keep it in place. I tie a crude bow. My injury looks like a Christmas present.

"Do you want us to stay here with you?" Amy asks.

"No," I say. "The night is young. I'll try to sleep. Maybe this is a bad dream." I try not to think of Florida. "Go, enjoy the rest of the party."

Steph flicks the light off. "If you need anything, shout."

"I'll scream like I'm being murdered."

I settle against the pillow and find a comfortable spot. I don't move my foot. The beer is nice. The pain is not. I finish the rest of my beer. I feel numb.

I grab my Blackberry. I open my thread of messages to Olivia and type "*I think I fucked up my foot, fuck my life*," with little precision. My fingers jab at the small keys. I click too many letters. I hit send.

The time on the home screen of my phone reads

11:00pm.

I shut my eyes. The pain continues.

Eventually, I pass out.

I wake up to a burst of pain. Faded sunlight creeps through the curtains across a small window near the ceiling. The display on my Blackberry reads 9:00am.

My head throbs.

My throat cracks.

My stomach churns.

My foot is *fucked*.

The swelling looks worse than I remembered. My entire ankle is swollen. The skin burns red. I shift my foot only slightly and bite down on my tongue to stop myself from screaming out loud in agony. *Deep breaths,* I tell myself. *It will be okay.*

I dial my home phone number on my Blackberry. A drawn out tone rings once, twice, and then the receiver on the other end clicks. "Hello?" says my mom.

"Hi Mom." My voice cracks. I start to cry.

"What's wrong?" she asks.

"I think I broke my foot."

Silence.

"You what?"

"I think I broke my foot."

Silence again.

"Matt…" she says. "What the fuck."

"Florida," I say simply.

"*Matt.*"

"They aren't going to let me on the rides at Harry Potter."

"Oh my god, Matt, what did you do?"

"I tripped."

"Were you drunk?"

Pause.

"No."

"Get yourself to a walk-in clinic. See if Amy or Steph will take you. Try to get an X-Ray. Maybe it's just sprained." She sighs. "Oh, Matt. Why aren't you more careful?"

"I am going to kill myself," I sob.

"*Shush.*"

"I'll let you know if I find out anything," I tell her. I sniffle. "Maybe you're right. Maybe it's just sprained."

"Or maybe you'll get a cast, and we'll have to rent a wheelchair and push you around Disney. They let the kids in wheelchairs go to the front of the line, you know."

I laugh.

"Be more careful, honey, okay?" Mom says. "Let me know when you see a doctor. I love you."

I tell her I love her too. I drop my phone to the ground and lean back against the pillow again.

I'm so stupid. I fucked up my trip.
I fall back asleep, crying.

ACKNOWLEDGMENTS

Thanks to everyone who has supported me. Never in my wildest of dreams would I have thought I'd be publishing my first (and hopefully not last) full-length book at twenty-two, so thank you to anyone who has ever shown me any support for my love of writing. To those who have helped me edit my work, to those who read my blog every time I spam Facebook, and to those who have told me in passing "Matt, you're a good writer," I am forever in debt to you. It means the world to me. I dedicate this book to you.

Thank you to my editing group: Melissa Carter, Tiff Limgenco, and Jenn Hoover. It's been a wild ride, but we all made it. I'm thankful for the kind words and the constructive edits you've given me throughout this process, and I am so proud of all of you.

Thank you to Guy Allen, one of the most influential professors I have ever had the privilege to learn under. You have taught me more about writing than you could ever know, and I am still to this day floored by the opportunity I have been given with this Making a Book class. A few years ago I told myself, "I will *never* take that book class." I'm so glad that I proved myself wrong. Thank you for the guidance and support.

A huge thank you to my parents. When I started university, I came as a Forensic Science student. I failed. I switched into English, and the switch into Professional Writing came a year later. Thank you, Mom and Dad, for supporting me even though you were hesitant about my new academic direction. I still don't know what I want to do (I might not ever know) but hey, I have a book.

Thank you to all of my friends, old and new, and to anyone who has ever shown me love in any way. To my friends back home in who I will love until I die, and to everyone I've grown to love at school (RLS, represent)—your care and support has meant everything to me. If I were to list names, I'd have another book on my hands; I will end by saying, I love and appreciate you all, and I will never be able to express into words the gratitude I feel for everything you have ever given me. Here's to the future.

Finally, thank you to anyone appearing in this book. There are some uncomfortable stories in here I thought I'd never revisit. In some cases, I've changed the names. In others, I haven't. Thank you to everyone. Even if we don't talk, even if you aren't now holding a copy of this book, know that you impacted me in some way and have helped me get to where I am now.

Thanks for the good times. And thanks for the fucking awful ones.

ABOUT THE AUTHOR

Now that this book has been completed and published, Matt Spadafora has absolutely nothing to talk about anymore.

He writes. He writes garbage, he writes some kind-of-good gems, but he writes everyday. He hopes to never stop.

Matt enjoys beer, pepperoni pizzas, and long walks on the beach.

33165322R00078

Made in the USA
Lexington, KY
15 June 2014